MIGHTY

The Story of an Oak Tree Ecosystem

*For Rachel Carson, one of my heroes.
You can see her on the back cover* —H. C.

Published by
PEACHTREE PUBLISHING COMPANY INC.
1700 Chattahoochee Avenue
Atlanta, Georgia 30318-2112
PeachtreeBooks.com

Text and illustrations © 2025 by Henry Cole

All rights reserved. No part of this publication may be reproduced, stored in a retrieval system, or transmitted in any form or by any means—electronic, mechanical, photocopy, recording, or any other—except for brief quotations in printed reviews, without the prior permission of the publisher.

Edited by Kathy Landwehr
Design and composition by Amy Manzo Toth
The illustrations were rendered using Micron pens on Bristol paper.

Printed in October 2024 by Leo Paper, Heshan, China.
10 9 8 7 6 5 4 3 2 1
First Edition
ISBN: 978-1-68263-733-3

Library of Congress Cataloging-in-Publication Data

Names: Cole, Henry, 1955- author, illustrator.
Title: Mighty : the story of an oak tree ecosystem / Henry Cole.
Description: Atlanta, Georgia : Peachtree Publishing Company Inc., [2025]
 Audience: Ages 4 - 8 | Audience: Grades K-1 | Summary: "This stunning, profound book explores the life cycle of a tree-not just through a season but across decades-as well as the other living things that depend upon it. How can something stay itself and yet change and grow? The oak tree shows us how"— Provided by publisher.
Identifiers: LCCN 2024031247 | ISBN 9781682637333 (hardcover)
 ISBN 9781682637708 (ebook)
Subjects: LCSH: Oak—Life cycles—Juvenile literature. | Oak—Ecology—Juvenile literature.
Classification: LCC QK495.F14 C64 2025 | DDC 583/.65—dc23/eng/20240705
LC record available at https://lccn.loc.gov/2024031247

EU Authorized Representative: HackettFlynn Ltd, 36 Cloch Choirneal, Balrothery, Co. Dublin, K32 C942, Ireland. EU@walkerpublishinggroup.com

MIGHTY
The Story of an Oak Tree Ecosystem

HENRY COLE

PEACHTREE
ATLANTA

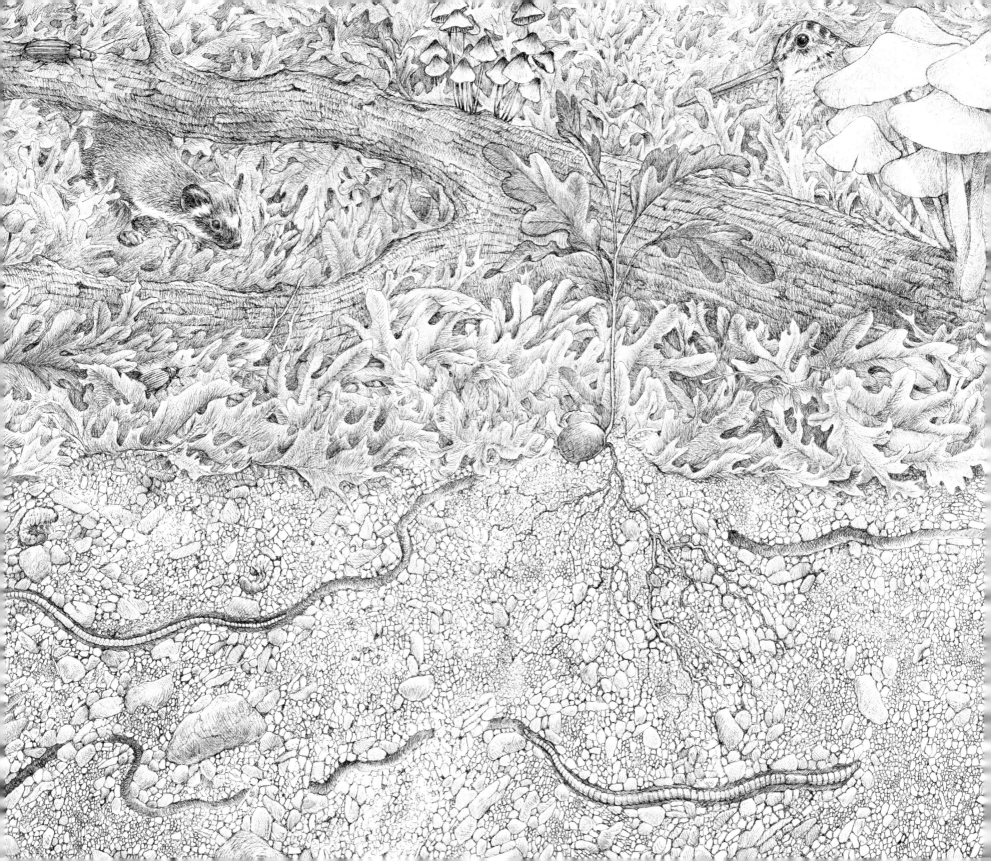

The acorn lands in a good spot. Days later,
it germinates, and an oak starts to grow.

With enough sunlight, rainfall, and nourishing soil, the seedling thrives. But even though it is bigger, it is still only a tiny part of a large forest floor.

A year passes.

The seedling becomes a sapling, its stems slender branches.

. . . and years later, taller still.

What began as the stalk of a seedling has become a sturdy trunk. Animals make their homes in the massive branches.

A century later, the tree towers over the forest floor.

Each spring, millions of insects are drawn to the tree's blossoms.

The blossoms develop into acorns, providing food for many animals. The summer night vibrates with songs of cicadas and katydids.

In the autumn, leaves turn brown and fall to the forest floor. Earthworms, fungi, and microorganisms and other decomposers enrich the soil. Migrating warblers rest in the oak as they journey south.

Winter. The tree may look lonely, but it is not alone. Squirrels take shelter in a nest made from dead leaves, perched high in the oak's branches.

Insects hide in crevices in the bark.
Chipmunks hibernate in tunnels among
the roots, nestled beneath the snow.

Humans are also drawn to the tree. In the heat of a summer day, they stop to rest in the cool shade.

Through the years, millions of acorns drop to the forest floor. Animals eat many of them. Others are damaged by insects.

The branches and leaves of the tree shade the ground, so most of the acorns that remain are unable to grow into seedlings.

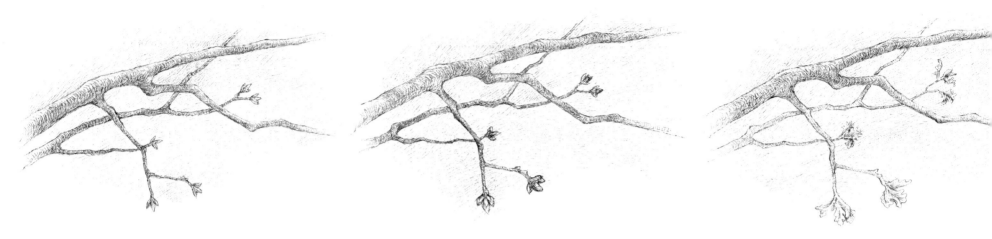

One spring, a pair of vireos finds the perfect spot to build a nest and raise their young.

The oak tree's leaves and branches provide camouflage for the nest, as well as a good supply of insects for food.

On his journey south, a naturalist stops to study the tree. "Remarkable specimen," he writes in his notes.

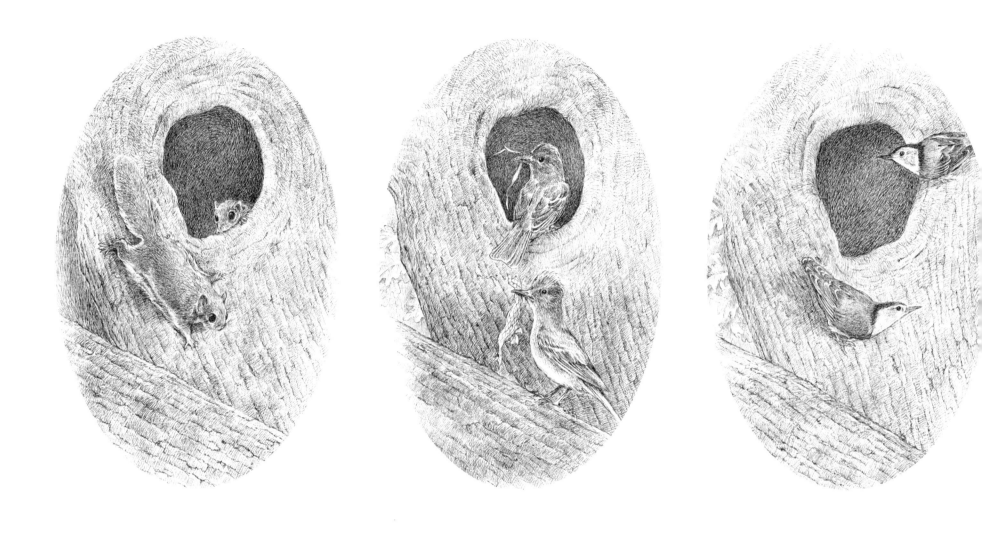

As the tree ages, a hole develops in a branch. Perhaps it was made by a woodpecker, or maybe a lightning strike. It becomes home to a family of flying squirrels.

Over the years, great crested flycatchers move in, followed by white-breasted nuthatches, screech-owls, raccoons, and wood ducks.

Humans build a home near the tree, which is nearly two centuries old. They use wood from many of the trees in the area.

Before long, other trees make way for another house.

What began as an acorn is now a mighty tree,
and a special part of a small town.

The tree is home.

How to Build an Ecosystem

An ecosystem is a relationship between plants and animals that interact and depend on each other. The mighty oak is the center of the ecosystem in this story. All the other plants and animals in the pictures are somehow dependent on the oak tree. Together, they create a habitat with a hugely diverse animal population. You need the following elements to create an ecosystem:

1. Start with a Producer

Like all plants, an oak is a producer. The chlorophyll in its leaves combines with carbon dioxide from the air and energy from sunlight to produce food so that it can grow. This process is called photosynthesis.

2. Add Consumers

Animals that cannot make their own food the way plants do are called consumers. These animals eat producers (or other consumers!). Some consumers are herbivores, which means they only eat producers. Some consumers only eat other consumers; they are called carnivores, or meat eaters. And finally, some consumers, like opossums and raccoons, will eat almost anything. They are called omnivores.

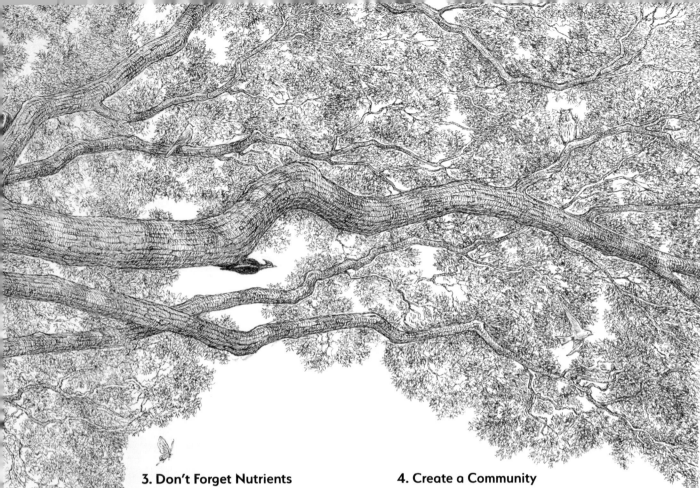

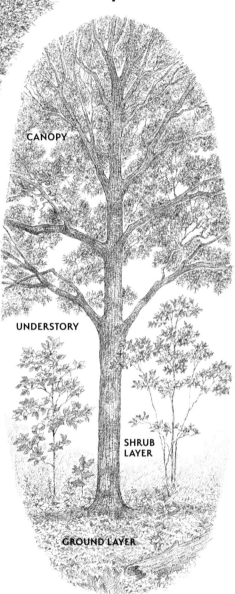

Forest Habitat Layers

CANOPY

UNDERSTORY

SHRUB LAYER

GROUND LAYER

3. Don't Forget Nutrients

An oak tree is deciduous, meaning its leaves drop every autumn. The fallen leaves provide food for an incredible number of organisms, from millipedes and earthworms to tiny bacteria and fungi. These are known as decomposers because they break down dead plants and animals, reducing them into nutrients that become food for plants.

4. Create a Community

A single mature oak tree is a habitat, a community of living things, each of which is in some way dependent on others. With its massive trunk and limbs, leafy branches, and bark filled with nooks and crannies, the oak tree offers nesting places and hiding spots for millions of animals. Many could not survive without its protection. The oak produces vast quantities of acorns (called "mast"), which provide food for many animals like deer, bears, chipmunks . . . and the blue jay that begins this story.

Jays bury thousands of acorns every fall for food storage for the winter months, but they don't remember all the locations. Sometimes when a jay forgets where it hid an acorn, it plants an oak tree for future generations of blue jays and other organisms. And future generations of people, too!